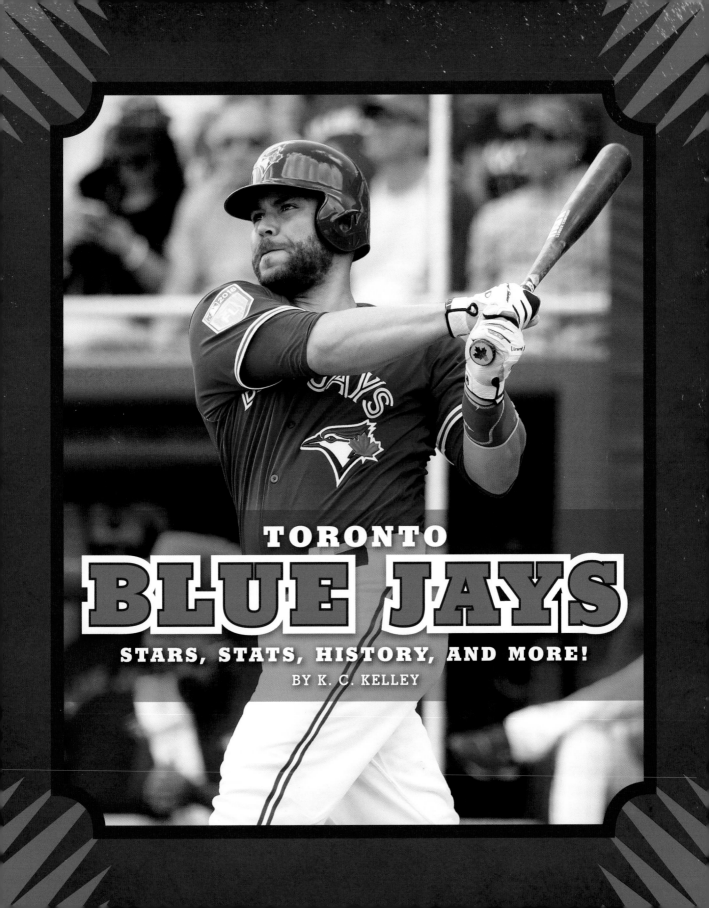

TORONTO
BLUE JAYS
STARS, STATS, HISTORY, AND MORE!
BY K. C. KELLEY

The Child's World®
childsworld.com

Published by The Child's World®
1980 Lookout Drive • Mankato, MN 56003-1705
800-599-READ • www.childsworld.com

ISBN 9781503828421
LCCN 2018944857

Printed in the United States of America
PAO2392

Photo Credits:
Cover: Joe Robbins (2).
Interior: AP Images: Hand Deryk, 17; Ed Kolenovsky 19,
Tony Tomsic 23; Alamy Stock: Design Pics Inc. 14; Katie
Buckley: 9; Dreamstime.com: Ffooter 12; Newscom: Nick
Wosika 6; Gerry Angus/Icon SW 10, Peter Llewlyn/Icon
SMI 20, Nick Wosicka/Icon SW 27; Joe Robbins 5, 29.

About the Author

K.C. Kelley is a huge sports
fan who has written more
than 100 books for kids. His
favorite sport is baseball.
He has also written about
football, basketball, soccer,
and even auto racing! He lives
in Santa Barbara, California.

On the Cover

Main photo: Catcher Russell Martin
Inset: Former home run hero
Carlos Delgado

CONTENTS

GO, BLUE JAYS!

et's talk baseball! Major League Baseball (MLB) is the top level of the sport. All MLB teams are in the United States, except one. The Toronto Blue Jays are the only team that plays in Canada. The Blue Jays have fans all over that nation (and in the United States, too)! Let's meet the Jays!

The red maple leaf in the Blue Jays logo is for Canada. ➤
It's worn here by outfielder Kevin Pillar.

WHO ARE THE BLUE JAYS?

he Blue Jays play in the American League (AL). That group is part of MLB. MLB also includes the National League (NL). There are 30 teams in MLB. The winner of the AL plays the winner of the NL in the **World Series**. The Blue Jays won the World Series in 1992 and 1993. Their fans look forward to another title soon!

◄ *Justin Smoak is Toronto's slugging first baseman.*

WHERE THEY CAME FROM

**M**LB added two new teams in 1977.
One of them was put in Toronto.
That city is in the Canadian **province**
of Ontario. Fans there were thrilled.
They even chose the team's name! More than 30,000
people sent in their ideas. The team's new owners
chose Blue Jays after a well-known bird.

These baseball cards came out in 1977, the Blue Jays' first season. ➤

WHO THEY PLAY

T he Blue Jays play in the AL East Division. The other teams in the AL East are the Baltimore Orioles, the Boston Red Sox, the New York Yankees, and the Tampa Bay Rays. The Blue Jays play more games against their division **rivals** than against other teams. In all, Toronto plays 162 games each season. They play 81 games at home and 81 on the road.

◄ *Aledmys Diaz throws over Boston's Mookie Betts to complete a double play.*

WHERE THEY PLAY

The Blue Jays play in one of baseball's coolest stadiums. It opened in 1989 and was called the SkyDome. It has a huge roof that can open and close on sunny days. A hotel is part of the building. Fans can watch the game from their rooms! In 2005, the SkyDome name was changed to Rogers Centre. (That's how they spell "center" in Canada!)

The curved roof of the Rogers Centre can ➤
close in case of rain . . . or snow!

THE BASEBALL FIELD

13 Carlos Garcia 2B

Is tied for 5 AL with six bunts this

OUTFIELD

FOUL LINE

FOUL LINE ◥

INFIELD

DUGOUT ▼

◥ FIRST BASE

▲ SECOND
BASE

ON-DECK
CIRCLE ▼

▲ PITCHER'S
MOUND

▲ HOME
PLATE

THIRD ▲
BASE

▲ COACH'S BOX

BIG DAYS

The Blue Jays have had a lot of great days in their short history. Here are a few of them.

1985—This was only their ninth season. The Blue Jays got one game away from the World Series! They won the AL East, but lost in the playoffs.

1992—Toronto became the first **foreign** team to win the World Series. They beat the Atlanta Braves. The Jays won the World Series again in 1993!

2015—For the first time since 1993, the Blue Jays won the AL East!

*Joe Carter leaps for joy in 1993. He had just hit ➤
a home run to win the World Series!*

TOUGH DAYS

**L**ike every team, the Blue Jays have had some not-so-great days, too. Here are a few their fans might not want to recall.

1979—The Blue Jays set a team record in their third season with 109 losses.

1981—Len Barker of the Cleveland Indians threw a **perfect game** against Toronto. Not a single Blue Jays batter reached base!

2000—The Blue Jays got crushed 23–1 by the Orioles. It was Toronto's worst loss ever. It even knocked them out of the playoff race!

The Blue Jays were on their backs often in 1979, losing 109 games. ➤

MEET THE FANS!

Blue Jays fans always pack their ballpark. In 1993, more than four million fans went to Blue Jays games. That was the third highest total ever for a season in MLB history! At the ballpark, fans enjoy seeing Ace. It's the team **mascot**. Fans all over Canada watch their home country's team on TV, too.

◄ *Ace works at the Rogers Centre to keep fans cheering for the Jays.*

HEROES THEN

The Blue Jays World Series teams had many great players. Second baseman Roberto Alomar made the **Hall of Fame**. Joe Carter was a slugging outfielder. Tony Fernandez played awesome defense at shortstop. In the 1990s and 2000s, Carlos Delgado had eight seasons with 30 or more homers. Dave Stieb holds most of the team's pitching records. He was a seven-time All-Star.

Dave Stieb played for the Blue Jays for 15 seasons. ➤

HEROES NOW

Today's Blue Jays include a mix of **veterans** and young stars. Third baseman First baseman Justin Smoak is a top slugger. Outfielder Teoscar Hernandez is a rising star. Kevin Pillar is one of the best defensive outfielders in MLB. Marcus Stroman is one of the Blue Jay's top pitchers.

◄ *Kendrys Morales is another great hitter for Toronto.*

GEARING UP

aseball players wear team uniforms. On defense, they wear leather gloves to catch the ball. As batters, they wear hard helmets. This protects them from pitches. Batters hit the ball with long wood bats. Each player chooses his own size of bat. Catchers have the toughest job. They wear a lot of protection.

THE BASEBALL

The outside of the Major League baseball is made from cow leather. Two leather pieces shaped like 8s are stitched together. There are 108 stitches of red thread. These stitches help players grip the ball. Inside, the ball has a small center of cork and rubber. Hundreds of feet of yarn are tightly wound around this center.

CATCHER'S MASK AND HELMET →

CHEST PROTECTOR →

CATCHER'S MITT

← SHIN GUARDS

CATCHER'S GEAR

TEAM STATS

Here are some of the all-time career records for the Toronto Blue Jays. All of these stats are through the 2018 regular season.

HOME RUNS	
Carlos Delgado	336
Jose Bautista	288

STOLEN BASES	
Lloyd Moseby	255
Roberto Alomar	206

BATTING AVERAGE	
Paul Molitor	.315
Roberto Alomar	.307

STRIKEOUTS	
Dave Stieb	1,658
Roy Halladay	1,495

WINS	
Dave Stieb	175
Roy Halladay	148

SAVES	
Tom Henke	217
Duane Ward	121

You'd smile, too, if you had a great career like Carlos Delgado. ➤

RBI	
Carlos Delgado	1,058
Vernon Wells	813

GLOSSARY

foreign (FOR-en) outside your home country

Hall of Fame (HALL UV FAYM) a building in Cooperstown, New York, that honors baseball heroes

mascot (MASS-cot) a costumed character who helps fans cheer

perfect game (PER-fekt GAYM) a game in which the starting pitcher wins and does not allow a single baserunner by the other team

province (PRAH-vince) name for a region of Canada much like a U.S. state

rivals (RYE-vuhlz) people or groups competing for the same thing

veterans (VET-er-enz) in sports, players with several years of experience

World Series (WURLD SEE-reez) the annual championship of Major League Baseball

FIND OUT MORE

IN THE LIBRARY

Connery-Boyd, Peg. *Toronto Blue Jays: The Big Book of Activities*. Chicago, IL: Sourcebooks, Jabberwocky, 2016.

Sports Illustrated Kids (editors). *The Big Book of Who: Baseball*. New York, NY: Sports Illustrated Kids, 2017.

Willis, John. *Toronto Blue Jays (Inside MLB)*. Calgary, AB: Weigl Publishers, 2017.

ON THE WEB

Visit our website for links about the Toronto Blue Jays:
childsworld.com/links

Note to Parents, Teachers, and Librarians: We routinely verify our web links to make sure they are safe and active sites. So encourage your readers to check them out!

INDEX